Shotgun Shopping

Also by Sheevaun O'Connor Moran

<u>Books</u>

Overcome the 7 Energies That Zap Your Life
Re-Write Your Prosperity Autobiography

<u>CD Programs</u>

Tropical Transformation
Woodsy Wonder
Violet Waterfall
Discover Your Divine Self
Reclaim Your Health
Weight Less
Living Wealthy & Prosperous
Clutter No More
Connect to Your Spirit and Soul
Essene Meditations
Kids Meditation
Master Your Energy Master Your Life Series

****

Please visit SheevaunMoran.com

Shotgun Shopping

How to Materialize Anything You Want
Through the Metaphor of Shopping

Metaphors, lessons, rules and inspiration on how to get
what you want through the metaphor of shopping.

This book empowers you to have what you truly want–
whether that's a designer pair of shoes, a new house,
a wedding dress, a baby grand piano, an apartment,
a relationship or what your imagination can conjure.

You will learn to save money, gain time and use the
Shotgun approach to materialize anything.

Sheevaun O'Connor Moran

Master Your Life Publishing

For information address:
Master Your Life Publishing,
P.O. Box 808, Huntington Beach, CA 92648.

Library of Congress Cataloging-in-Publication Data:
O'Connor Moran, Sheevaun
Shotgun Shopping: How to Materialize Anything You Want Through
the Metaphor of Shopping / Sheevaun O'Connor Moran

ISBN 978-0-9819521-0-9

1. Self actualization   2. Change (Psychology)   3. Mind and Body

Sheevaun O'Connor Moran websites

www.ShotgunShoppingBook.com
www.SheevaunMoran.com
www.MasterYourEnergyMasterYourLife.com

Dedication

This is dedicated to my mother, the shopper of all shoppers. Even when she wasn't shopping for anything, she went shopping. As she will never get to read these pages about how she shaped me and my shopping abilites, she shaped my love of wonderful deals, her shopping sprees taught me to be clear and get what I want and get out fast. She won't know, that I know, she showed her love by remembering every event with a card (that she shopped for and always noted what a great deal she got). I send her love and laughter and lots of good shopping excursions.

This work is also dedicated to all those people I have ever encountered, wanting to know where I got what I was wearing, who inspired the term "Shotgun Shopping."

TABLE OF CONTENTS

Introduction   10

The Evolution of How I became a Non-Shopper   18

Confessions of a Non-Shopper!   24

Why You Might Want to Be a "Shotgun Shopper"   36

Shoes Mini Lessons—Everyone Needs Shoes!   38

A Witness to the Non-Shopping Madness Gives Testimony   40

What do Shoes and the Dalai Llama Have in Common?   44

Rules:

Make a List—Yes You   48

Know How Much You Want to or Can Spend   58

How Much Is Your Time Worth   66

Follow Your Instincts—Trust   72

Don't Get the Salesperson Involved   80

Do Not Shop with the Shop-a-holic Type   86

Decree That You Will Not Need to Return Things   92

Know the Details—Before Leaving the House   100

Best Times to Avoid Any Shopping—Period!   106

Best Times to Shop; No Really the Best Times to Shop   114

Mall Shopping   120

Tips for a Great End to the Non-Shopping Adventure   124

Shopping Karma   128

The Golden Rule Is; Give and You Shall Receive   134

Stories How to Use This Aversion to Your Advantage   136

Notes   144

"Shotgun Shopping" is Really Manifesting   146
What you Want, Wish, and Desire

Introduction

When I walk through my home, I am easily reminded of hundreds of stories from items purchased or acquired and what I did to "not shop" to buy each item. The reason for this is that I cannot stand shopping. Can't even stand the word shopping. Can't even stand when I need to go to the market, because that constitutes shopping. I often wait until there is nothing left in my kitchen and I've been as creative with food as Mother Hubbard ever was—just so I don't have to shop.

Ok, so you get the picture, shopping and I have a rocky relationship. While there are books about how to shop, how to cure yourself of shopping too much—books about how to get the best deal, at Neiman's basement sale, I felt it was high time that we acknowledge the other un-heralded group—NON-shoppers. You've probably heard of a few people who fit into this group, maybe you've even known a NON-shopper. Most men will tell you they are non-shoppers, but I've discovered that this is only partly true, as most men will spend a great deal of time shopping for the right gadget, with the right features and in just the right color.

Actually, there are more NON-shoppers than you can imagine. We sit and listen when others talk about their full day of shopping. Our faces may show interest but we're gazing off and working on a subject change. We find any excuse to avoid shopping. When asked to join someone on a shopping excursion we've already got plans. Whether we need to go to that particular store or not at that moment, it

never seems like the right time. We just won't go shopping.

Though hard-core shopping is necessary in some situations, you will discover that it is completely unnecessary in most. Life is full of things to want and to buy and whether you spend your hard earned money, I mean credit, on them is entirely up to you. There will always be the need for going to the supermarket (I'm going to vow that some day going to the supermarket will be okay with me). For now I say, "Why take so much time in the hunting phase? Why not know how to be laser focused and use a non-shopping ~ materializing ~ technique?"

You will also discover that life is like a constant adventure in materializing what you desire. Using the shotgun analogy to hone your shopping prowess will allow you to have a better understanding of this "non-shopping" methodology?

Do we just go out and spend thousands of dollars on cars without being clear about what we want before we make the purchase?

In most situations in order to get what we want we need to have some clarity, particularly when purchasing a car. Why not do the same with all your shopping needs? Why settle for less than what you want or desire? Why spend so much time in the hunting phase?

Shotgun Shopping is nothing more than a different way of

looking at what our ancestors did in the early human days –hunting and gathering. Really, shopping is the same as what our ancient ancestors did when they needed to thrive and survive. Ok, maybe this is somewhat of a stretch, but in essence what you do when you shop is hunt, hunt, hunt. When you make the purchase, that's the gathering piece. For most people today shopping is like going out into the wild but without knowing what it is you are hunting for, expecting to make that special purchase. Shopping for exactly what you want, without specifics, is like a hunter going out with a shotgun—moving through the thick forest he has the intent of finding something, anything—to bring home, only coming home empty-handed.

Just like a hunter during moose season goes hunting for moose and not hunting for duck, shopping should be performed with specific intent. Maybe we should go so far as calling certain times of the year shoe season, or skirt season. Anyway, you see my point.

This book is about taking the "hunting for everything" concept and bringing focus to your desired target while teaching you to become a master at manifesting, materializing and gathering exactly what you want from your shopping needs.

My approach is to take those inborn hunting desires and hone them to gain, using techniques that will achieve the acquisition that is <u>best of the best</u>. These techniques will not only help you purchase exactly what is right for you, but also help you keep <u>only</u> what is right. Buying anything less than exactly what you want is wrong and if this does happen, those items should not enter your home through these techniques.

Also, I'm going to share some important tips, tricks, and anecdotes that will help the shoppers, the wanna be non-shoppers and will help the over-shoppers become efficient. If you're reading this then you've got at least someone in mind that needs help with his or her shopping adventures. The plethora of store choices are simplified for you–the rules and exercises in this book are simple and to the point–resulting in a little book you will want to keep, or hide in your purse on your next excursion.

"Shotgun Shopping" is for anyone in the world whether you're on home turf or traveling. The techniques are even designed to help those who over accumulate, I mean collect clutter, to take steps to clear out some of that "stuff". If you are the type who is faint of heart and unwilling to even consider a new way of shopping, then just read these pages and enjoy the stories. Maybe you will learn a trick or two and find new ways to apply some of the techniques to other areas of your life.

One of the aspects of this book, is that it won't matter what the object of your desire is—all the rules and techniques apply. No matter what you wish for—a home, a car or just an overpriced pair of shoes where you pay 1/4 of the retail price—know that all these rules and tips can be applied in the same manner. I even had a client who used these techniques to find a boyfriend.

Shhh, don't tell everyone how you learned these tips, but if you see someone who has this problem, rip a page from the back that has some key information and proudly give it to them. Or you might just want to grab a few copies and share them with your neighbors; you know the ones with the overstuffed garage, maybe even anonymously. And, as I've got so many stories to tell about non-shopping purchases, I will share some of those in hopes of inspiring you to achieve true non-shopping status. The stories I'm going to share are true and do not use any of the characters or brands real names in an effort to protect the innocent, mainly me.

I look forward to hearing some of your non-shopping, "Shotgun Shopping" stories and how you materialized the mundane. One reader told me recently, "I went to Costco and was overwhelmed. I decided to get clear about the need for someone to help me, and used the Shotgun Shopping techniques right there in the middle of the store. Next thing I know this young, handsome, man was there and helped me all the way out to my car."

There is often comraderie in sharing and learning through the successes and mistakes of others. There is also great joy in writing down the successes you've had in addition to the recollection of interesting stories. As a result you make the story that much easier to happen repeatedly.

Let me know how fast you materialized / manifested something. Tell me that you were able to get your hearts' desire and the funky story that led to it happening.

These techniques are for you, so go and Shotgun Shop and get EXACTLY what you want.

Send your stories to author@SheevaunMoran.com

The Evolution of How I Became a Non-Shopper!

Where I grew up there were a few shops in the middle of town and when we needed to go shopping, for the real big purchases, it was an excursion. In case this is something that's hard to believe, the population of the town was less than 5,000. It had 3 clothes stores, 2 record stores, 1 hardware store, 1 furniture store..., well you get the picture. Shopping for anything was a unique experience. A few of the larger stores were on the outskirts of town and anything beyond that required an excursion. Now, I liked excursions and loved to be away from home, but it seems that the only part I remember liking about shopping, was the drive to and from home. My mother took us on a lot of shopping excursions. Little did I know that this was her way of staying in touch with the world and escaping the small town atmosphere.

My mother was a fashion hound and loved to go on these excursions. She grew up without a lot. Her mother made her clothes but they were designer beautiful clothes. Her love of shopping also came from being raised with easy access to the city, as well as working in her 20's in the city, with access to the best shops and discounts. She was one of those working-women who provided for herself and didn't get married until she was 30 years old, somewhat of a scandal in the 50's. She married my dad and they lived close to large cities for the first few years. Eventually my parents moved to a tiny town without much to offer in the way of shops, culture or much of anything else for that matter.

My mother was inventive with ways to take excursions on her own and then she became inventive in other ways, taking her children along for the ride. We would drive 12-30 miles to find areas where there were lots of shops. At the time this seemed so far to go just to have to go shopping. The only mall seemed even further away but it was only about 40 minutes away. She spent hours taking us, I mean dragging us, from store to store to find just the right selection of clothes. She also wanted to ensure that we had nothing like the other kids in town and that each article was the best in quality. It had to be a good bargain or else she wouldn't buy it and if we found something we actually liked and it wasn't in her budget, she would cleverly direct us to something else she had in mind that fit her budget.

Nevertheless, my mother loved to shop. Later in her life she was told to walk a lot more and where did she go? She went to the mall, to window shop and get her walking quota.

For me shopping just meant having to be confined in a building and searching endlessly for something that was different. My mother was queen at finding expensive clothes that were amazing deals. To this day I don't know how she did it given the financial limitations she lived under. That mindset just made me learn how to hone in on exactly what I wanted at the price I needed.

Shopping felt like slow torture. Not only was I confined to a building, but it also meant that I would have to settle for my mother's idea of what I wanted. It felt as if we spent days going through racks of stuff and from store to store. I recall going to the other side of the store and just wandering around, when I felt I had been gone a while I would peek my head over the racks and look for her red hair, to see where in the process of this torture we were. Was she at the check-out counter yet? I would flick through the racks of clothes and pick what I was interested in, try it on, and give it to mom for the purchase; I would quickly then ask if we could go. I remember asking, frequently, if I could go outside after we'd made a few purchases and wait for everyone. It's apparent, looking back, that the time spent shopping was definitely not one of my favorite pastimes.

Shotgun Shopping

I was one of those most would call a tomboy. But the truly hilarious part was, that I wasn't allowed to own a pair of jeans and so I was a well-dressed tomboy. I wasn't permitted to leave the house without looking nice. God forbid that I should ever be seen wearing dungarees (jeans for those who don't know or remember). Before there were fashion police and Cosmo Don'ts, there was my mother. If I didn't look perfect before leaving the house, then I had to change.

My parents were ones who wanted the best for their children. They weren't going to allow certain changes that the world was undergoing, to get into their lives or change their idea of what image they wanted their children to portray.

Growing up in such a small town did make buying things easy in one sense but extremely challenging in the developing a love for shopping sense. All I had to do was divert my walk home from school, uphill and 1.8 miles in the snow, through the middle of town. Not really kidding about the walking home but I don't really think it was 1.8 miles, it was probably more like 20 miles. If I was in need of something, of course not too extravagant and something that someone else in town might have, all I needed to do was to go into a shop and pick something out and say put it on our account. Get this; I didn't even need money because it was such a small town that we had an account at most of the stores, except the grocery store. This sounds surreal today, I know, but I only had to be careful not to spend too much to stay under the radar. Little did I realize at the time I could have gone hog wild, but funny thing I never did, I just bought what was needed or what I really, really wanted.

Here's this other aspect of growing up that I think shaped my non-shopping status. I was the first girl in town to have a lawn-mowing route. I mowed lawns for as many of the neighbors as I could and was paid very nicely. In the winter I had a snow-shoveling route, although I didn't like that one as much. As it was, I made good money and began putting it into a savings account. *Something we all need for our adventures in materializing.* Any time that I really wanted something that was not on the approved list, I bought it with my own money. I think this left an impression on the shopping neurons in my brain and has been one of the contributing factors to my shopping avoidance. It was about spending my own money and because I had to earn it on my own, I was able to buy what I wanted. I would factor in that I wanted just the right item and pay what I had allotted.

Confessions of a Non-Shopper!

You would think that I run around in rags and have old things or things that don't match or that will just make due, but the truth of the matter is that I love **beautiful**, new things. With a mother as the fashion police, I did come away without too much rebellion and a love of well-made things that are often expensive. My non-shopping status may also give you pause to think that I have scant few things to select from in my wardrobe, when in reality I have a closet and a half full of clothes. I wear all items in my closet (as a rule) and love to purchase new items. It could be thought that I won't spend a lot of money on items but that is not entirely true. You may also think that I never step foot into a store. But as you will soon see this also is not true, I just don't spend much time in them.

I've been successful at buying nearly all of my clothes, shoes (and yes I do have a lot of shoes), office furniture, and home decor without "shopping". The other truth of the matter is that I love expensive things and yet refuse to spend exorbitant sums of money on something just to fill the space or the need. Impossible, you might say, but I say there's a methodology to how you can thrive and survive and have beautiful things without shopping. You can also have beautiful things at a great price if you are willing to think and operate outside of the shopping norm.

While writing the chapters for this book it made me reflect, taking walks down the journey of each acquisition and the sometimes very funny ways I've been able to acquire items throughout my life, with as little "shopping" as possible. Even when I lived in the city I didn't shop. I used the techniques from growing up, to shop or make a quick purchase on the way home, so it didn't seem like shopping tactic. Now that I think of it, that's how my entire wardrobe came about while working in the city. So when I moved to California, shopping first meant having to go to a mall and developing, to the finest detail, the "Shotgun Shopping" method.

Most of my life people would make comments on something I was wearing or something that I had in my home and ask where I bought it. They would often say "when you're done with that you can just give it to me." Just the other day I was stopped in the parking lot on the way to my car and asked about some silk pants I was wearing. (They were black silk Capri style and the sides were sculpted cut outs from the bottom to mid thigh with the ties at the bottom drooped in a lazy bow. I'd never seen anything like them, dressy yet casual). The woman took one of those double takes and then literally marched after me, complimented me on my outfit and particularly the pants and then asked where I bought them. Because I don't often go to the same stores or recall where purchases are made, I told her I didn't remember. We talked for a bit about where to find different clothes and I told her "Oh I use the "Shotgun Shopping" method". She laughed and wanted to know more. When I respond with this statement, some people tilt their head and give a quizzical look, but mostly people get it right away. Sometimes I will ask if they want to hear about how I came across it. Of course, the story is really a mini adventure and a seeming miracle as to how this beautiful whatever came to be in my hands. The story about the store or item never needs to be exaggerated. The next thing that usually happens is that they would want to share how they make their purchases. I guess this is like sharing around the campfire after the hunting is done–type story sharing. They would proceed to tell me how much they love, love, love shopping and where they go and on and on and on. But now, in most cases, I've learned to skip the story.

One of the most interesting pieces of this non-shopping scenario is that there are a lot of stores that I've only gone into once. Of course I don't remember the name of the store but often I can give details about how to find that particular store.

There was an occasion recently when a friend of mine wanted to buy a number of new plants for her house. I had found this amazing place to buy the best plants at amazingly low prices and mentioned it to her. When she called to get the address I was on a road trip and had a few hours to get to my destination, so I stayed on the phone with her directing her into the exact area and building without her ever needing to know the address or even knowing the name of the place.

I suppose all of this could mean that I get bored easily. I think it has to do with my parents telling me as a child that I should dress and look and be different than everyone else. We've all heard the phrase "would you jump off a bridge if your friends did?" Of course this really was meant to shape us to think differently. It did shape me and resulted in me being a non-shopper.

I don't remember exactly when I decided that shopping was evil but I do remember a few very important moments when I realized that I didn't like to shop. It took me most of my life to realize this complete dislike of shopping and one of the ways I've discovered it is through people wanting my secret to non-shopping (acquiring what I want at the price I want) and the writing of this book.

There was a time during my first marriage that it became apparent to my husband that I didn't like shopping so he would make a point to go to the store with me. We would even go so far as to set up dates for going to the supermarket otherwise there would be no food in the house.

I remember one Christmas that we needed to finish our gift purchases and he wanted to go to the mall. He really wanted me to go because we needed to finish getting presents for both our families. The mall is one of those places that—well I'll get into that one later. We had a list and had designated about 2 hours to get everything done. It was taking a lot longer than the 2 hours because he wanted to check out every new gadget that could improve his/our life. He was carrying the bags from our purchases and I was dragging behind telling him I needed to eat, I needed to go sit down—anything to stop the store wandering. I finally decided I'd had enough and rather than rain on his parade, I went to find a tree inside the mall and sit. So here I was the only woman sitting in the middle of the mall, like many men do, waiting for my husband to finish his shopping. He LOVED shopping and so he spent hours at the mall when he was in need of new things.

Each year for special events I would make a list of about 35 things that I wanted and gave the list to him so that he could really shop. This method was so I would end up being surprised at the final gift.

Ladies in case you missed this one, it's a great way to get your guy to give you exactly what you want.

This method ensured I didn't have to buy my own things and I would get exactly what I wanted while he got the joy of spending hours, hunting for the perfect thing that was somewhere on the list. It also meant that he could buy whatever he wanted without having to ask what I thought. This little tip could mean that you end up with all the items on the list, but what fun would that be?

Of course I didn't realize that he had actually saved me from the drudgery of shopping, until much later. After he had passed, unexpectedly, it became apparent how much I didn't like to shop because I never had much of anything to eat in the house. To remedy this, my mother and I worked out a schedule where she would go shopping with me. She wanted to take coupons and make me buy what was on sale even though it wasn't what brand or size I wanted. Boy was that a challenge, as I had been the one pushing the cart and making the quick decisions in the past, so we could get in and out in record time. This time shopping with my mother made me learn how to shop for things all over again. So I made it a game to see how fast I could get into the store, get my mother to agree with my selection even though I didn't have a coupon, and out with all the things I needed. It took some time but I then realized that I had already been using this "game" to buy clothes and furniture and many acquisitions throughout my life.

I then took a corporate job that required a lot of travel and that is when the fine details of the "Shotgun Shopping" method were born. This was a job where I would be on a trip for 5-10 days with several stops across the country. In the beginning I tried to travel like men, but being 5'3", not able to lift as much as men while needing more clothes than men, nearly crippled me with all the lugging and lifting of carry-on garment bags. I wanted to travel with as little as possible and I needed to have the essentials with me so that I could function. If I didn't, then I would have to find some way to make a stop and a quick purchase. In the early stages of the trips I burned a good deal of midnight oil ensuring I had everything I needed, it was somewhat easy to keep up. But after a few years things just seemed to get left out and I would be without a pair of pants to a suit or a blouse that wouldn't match any of the outfits I brought. There were also the times when it was freezing cold when it was supposed to be warm and vice versa. I fortunately had the attitude of "Well then I would simply have to find a store somewhere to buy what was needed". The less frustrated I was, the easier it was to find what I needed, in the nick of time—this was an early on discovery.

It's funny because the first company I started, on my own, was a catalog company for people who travel a lot. It ensured that they didn't have to go somewhere to shop, for the travel size necessities of life on their business travels. My company objective was to provide products for those on the road, things that they had forgotten or didn't have time to go shopping to buy. Of course at the time I didn't realize the extent of my anti-shopping attitude and attributed it to not having enough time. I made the assumption that all people who travel a lot don't like to or don't have time to "go shopping". Because I didn't like to go to malls or shop, I put together a new concept catalog for travel and trial size products. This was before every drugstore, mall shop or airport store, began carrying trial size products. Small travel size products and accessories were difficult to find.

There are two times that come to mind when having the right items were more difficult to resolve. One was when I was flying to a meeting in Oklahoma and after a freak snowstorm my flight was delayed. I landed about 9:30 pm, made it to the hotel to unpack and realized that I had 3 suits for 5 days and only had the jackets and blouses to the suit and the pants and skirts were missing. So that next day I went to my meeting in a suit jacket and jeans. I got the business, but it was interesting to explain it to the customer. To recover from that one, I had a friend go to my house and get the bottom half of the suits and overnight them to the next city. The next very memorable time was on a trip several years later that was for 5 days and it was a 6-hour drive to the location. I realized about half way there that I'd left every item of clothes that I was going to need for my seminars on the banister at home. They'd just come back from the dry cleaner. The only items I had with me were my personal items. This story is a classic example of "Shotgun Shopping" as I raced into town, held the class, and told my friend what I'd done. She whisks me off to the most expensive place in the city and I'm saying to myself "this is going to cost me a lot of money to replace everything". So I bought two items that I just couldn't live without in about 20 minutes and then told my friend to drop me off at my car.

I then raced to this other mega outlet center and found 7 designer items and only paid about $150 for all 7. My technique on this one was pray, pray, envision, pray, pray. Just kidding, but I did decide that I had a limited amount of money and only about two hours before having to be at the next event as well as the need for 5 days of outfits. Actually it worked out so well I still have some of those pieces, because they are classic and go with anything.

Most people border on the "shop-a-holic, need to stop spending path" but you won't find my footprints on the shopping path. Now let's get started with some of how I "non-shop", I know you'll have some fun and try the "Shotgun Shopping" method after you read this book.

One of the solutions to "not shop" is to hire someone else to shop for you. And you laugh! Most of us, myself included, are not ladies/men of leisure with our own private butler, but there's no reason we shouldn't dream about this possibility. Dreams sometime lead to reality, so why not dream. Through this method all you would have to do is say I love it or no thank you. Then you won't even have to go to a store once let alone twice. I'm sure that you know I would love this one but truthfully, it is the conquest and non-attachment to the outcome that makes "Shotgun Shopping" so ideal for me. It's also because I'm not so good at communicating the colors and pictures in my mind to others. The universe may have something even more wonderful in mind than my image and I might miss out on that opportunity. The butler scenario would take the fun out of the really getting what you want and the fun out of the non-shopping success.

As you may have guessed by now, the reality of the situation is that you will need to do most of your own buying activity. Most people would use the word "work" but I use the word activity because we have so much dread surrounding that word "work". The last thing we need is another negative word in our lives such as "work".

Why You Might Want To Be a "Shotgun Shopper"

For many, shopping is a release and a pleasure. Some hope to fill a void when shopping. Many use it as a mechanism to interact with others. For other's it's stressful and frustrating. There is also another group that shop to keep up with the Joneses. I say there is nothing wrong with you if you are a shopper, really, I admire someone who can shop. I say there's nothing wrong with you in any of these situations, but I say let's stop for a moment and see if we can't make this shopping thing better.

Even if you don't convert to the "Shotgun Shopping" way you may learn a few things about how to make your "time" work for you and your acquisitions to be more in line with what you want. You may learn to curb your appetite and make "as needed" purchases rather than "it makes me feel better in the moment" purchases. You may learn how to use the tools and techniques to manifest in other areas of your life.

Shoes, Mini Lessons— Everyone Needs Shoes!®

It seems that most women on the planet, well at least in the civilized world, love shoes. Remember Imelda Marcos of the Philippines? I actually saw her in a hotel recently and she looked pretty normal to me. She became an icon just because her shoe addiction was discovered, when most women go around quietly collecting their own shoe fortune (I mean collection). Shoes are no less a passion for me. Although I no longer use extreme shoe collecting as a hobby, I do have a shoe style for just about any occasion.

Shoes are the ideal item because they are easy to buy on the fly and a perfect example of how "Shotgun Shopping" works. They are small, portable and can be tried on in the quickest manner. All you have to do is slip your shoes off, of course while standing, and try one on that looks to be your size on display. Also shoes are specific to the taste and comfort of the wearer. So if the shoe fits only buy it—if you really need it and it's exactly what you want as well as the price you want to pay and in your budget.

A Witness to the Non-shopping Madness Gives Testimony

I had the privilege to witness this "Shotgun Shopping" for myself. It wasn't until I had been with Sheevaun a few times that I truly understood the method to her madness. The day it clicked for me was in a shoe store on the way back from lunch.

As we walked through a promenade of boutiques and wonderful stores on the way to the car, one store caught her eye. Shoes! She loves shoes. We walked in and headed straight for the shoes. Carefully inspecting the quality of the shoe, she tried on the display model. The keen eye of the salesperson spotted it was a tight fit and promptly replied, "Can I bring you a pair from the back in your size?" Of course the answer was a resounding "Yes." So off the sales woman went. As she was in the back, Sheevaun quickly scanned the rest of the store for any other possibilities.

The salesperson arrived shortly with the right size. She tried on the shoes and found that even the right size was not what she wanted. At this time I'm standing and looking at the shoes the salesperson is putting back in the box and listening to their conversation.

"Would you like to try another pair?"

At this point Sheevaun's voice seemed more faint.

"No thank you."

I turned around and Sheevaun had slipped on her shoes and was already out the door. My jaw dropped. I looked at the salesperson and said with a smile, "I guess we'll be going now." I assumed we were going to spend more time in the store, since her love for shoes was great. Very important lesson, I don't assume anymore and stand ready to go because this is "Shotgun Shopping."

What do Shoes and the Dalai Lama Have in Common?

Well the Dalai Lama and shoes really have no common ground, particularly since Buddhists don't allow people to wear shoes in their homes or places of worship — except that I happened to be given a ticket to see him in person. The tickets stated clearly that you could not be late or you wouldn't be allowed into the theater until a later session. So living in LA and having a lot to accomplish in any given day, as you can imagine, I got on the road a few minutes late. I figured it was the middle of the day and I'd have no problem getting there in 40 minutes and that there should be no traffic. Of course this is LA and getting from point A to point B is a crapshoot, as the freeways and traffic are never predictable.

It was a beautiful sunny day, warmer than usual for late spring, I needed to go back home to get a sweater in case it got cold in the theater, I did not want to sit and freeze for hours listening to the Dalai Lama. It turns out that I'm about an hour late for the first session and 40 minutes early for the second session. I sat in my car making calls, arranging my day and week and organizing everything I could get my hands on. I then decided to find a better parking space. Discovering an outdoor mall I thought I'd get something to eat. I parked in the closer space and made my way across the street to grab a snack. As I turned the corner I spotted this fabulous shoe store, breezed in and ended up trying on a few pairs of shoes. None that I loved, so I decided to make my purchase of tea and a muffin, when I spotted another store with one pair of shoes in the window that were just too

45

cute. I raced in and tried them on. **THEY FIT, I LOVED THEM, I NEEDED THEM, THEY WERE EXACTLY WHAT I HAD IN MIND FOR A FEW OUTFITS,** but how could I take a pair of just purchased shoes in their box into the security line to see the Dalai Lama? I decided to wait and buy them later. Well I didn't get back to that store that day to buy those special shoes. The moral of this story is that you should buy exactly what fits and you love at the time of the find. It took me another 2 weeks to locate the shoes in my size and at that I had to have them shipped. This was quite contrary to the full "Shotgun Shopping" methodology. I decided not to make the purchase at the time but hey, my spiritual life was more important than a pair of very cute shoes.

What do Shoes and the Dali Lama Have in Common?

Rule Number 1
—Make a List—Yes You

Iknow, I know, I know, everyone says make a list. Yes, lists can get out of control and you can make endless lists and never even look at them. A lot of people do this. But this time you **really** do need to make a list of things that you want, wish, or need. You may say that you have the list in your head. But there are a lot of other things in your head and does that really mean that you'll get them all done? Does it mean that you will get exactly what you need? Does it mean that you get it when you need it or want it? Making a list allows the universe, and your brain, to completely grasp and get a hold of what it is that is desired, so that the universe can bring that item to you more easily and more quickly.

Consider this list your master list and (*here's the key*) then beside each item listed write the highest amount you are willing to pay for that item. Then write beside that "or less" or a minus sign. This can be the biggest list you've ever made but make it one that has clarity and certainty about the end purchase. It's all about how clear you are.

Another important item usually left off is the dollar ($) sign when referring to price. Our brain doesn't understand that a number is for dollars unless you place that all important $ sign beside it. It's no joke, please remember to write in a $ sign beside the item on the list. Again, the $ sign is often forgotten and then all you have is a number without the attachment to the dollars you are willing or going to spend.

You will notice that I've said write and I didn't say type. You really need to hand write this list on a clean sheet of paper that is lined. Yellow is the best. There's a lot to be said about the force and energy behind something that is handwritten.

CAUTION: At this early phase of using these techniques, refrain from using your computer to make the list. It won't have the same impact or result in the fastest materialization possible.

To capture the most energy, which helps to manifest, writing with pen and paper is your best bet. Only when you get to be a pro at list mastery and materializing is when you can begin to use the computer for your list. I'd say wait until you've practiced this technique for about 6 months so that it's thoroughly ingrained in your brain.

Again, until you are a list master it is necessary to handwrite your list.

Example:

| Manolo Blanick, shoes - pink | $125 or less |
| Leather sofa | $600 or less |

I've tried both writing it on paper and typing it into the computer and while I've been perfecting these techniques for several years my best results came from having written it on paper. After many years I now type them onto the top of my "To Do List" and make it bold and retype it frequently. But, if things aren't moving along quickly enough then I revert back to handwriting using the pen and paper.

Once you have a clear picture of what you need and the money associated with each item then you can move on, to the real fun. I say real fun because here's where I'm going to make you stretch yourself. This is where you will need to use something that is usually not easy "trust yourself". We have these two words that seem to go hand in hand they are trust yourself and then somehow second guess gets tacked on. Usually this is because of past training. Those words, second guess, need to move out of the same apartment and now is a good time to become friends with "trust yourself".

Here's a simple exercise to begin to learn and I really mean just begin to learn to "trust yourself". For 24 hours follow your instincts about where you're supposed to be, so long as it's a positive action. Trust is a funny thing and when we know better and yet don't trust ourselves we end up saying "Oh if only I had twenty twenty hindsight". We'll share a rule and some techniques on how to be better at trusting yourself later in the book.

Not to give you any ideas about getting off the hook for

making a list but here's something that might help. Remember everything about the things you should have put on the list to the most minute detail. Remember the priority and remember the dimensions. Without a list on paper you're going to have to go to Evelyn Wood memory school so that you remember the item, color, and other details and most importantly what your highest amount to spend on that item would be. Since most people talk about how bad their memory is and that they need ginkgo biloba, I say just break out a sheet of paper and review the above steps for making your list.

Review

√   Yellow lined paper
√   Handwrite list of wishes or wants
√   Include $$ sign written beside each item
√   Add the words "or less" after each wish

Special note to remember: Writing has more power than speaking because you, your conscious and unconscious brain, and the universe will all have a clear understanding of items or the ultimate desire. They will all be on the same page, so to speak. When you make the space for something to comeinto your life, then the universe can bring something that you truly desire much more easily and more quickly.

Anecdotes about Making a List

I moved from a home I'd been living in for 6 years and during the planning of the move I made a decision to get rid of all furniture except a kitchen table and 1 chair. My clothes also had to go, and so I let go of a lot of my closet contents, including shoes. This was with the intention of having a fresh outlook, a fresh start, in the new house. Little did I know I was testing my ability to use lists and acquire what was needed through "Shotgun Shopping". I moved into this large home without even owning a bed. I was sleeping on the floor the first night and thought, "Wow, what was I thinking? I guess I went a little overboard, didn't I?"

Leather sofa

After giving most everything away and a fresh outlook, I only kept the artwork that I loved and slightly more than 70% of my clothes, a table and chairs, a carpet and one lounge chair. This meant that I had to fill the house with new things and one of the aspects of this that never came into my mind, until I had already moved in, was that I didn't like to shop. It took me a while living in the huge empty space to decide how I wanted things to look, but after a few months I set about making a master list of what I needed, wished for, and desired.

I used the technique of writing what was in my budget first, even though some of the numbers seemed unrealistically low. When I tallied the numbers of these items I was in shock and slight discomfort as to how it was going to work out that I would get one piece of furniture, let alone a whole house full of new furniture.

I had nothing for guests to sit on except the floor and after a small gathering I'd had where the guests had to bring their own fold up chairs, I decided to move the leather sofa that I had desired, to the top of the list. In the process I had received a Saturday paper delivered to my doorstep (I don't subscribe to the newspaper) and for some reason I paged through the paper with no specific intent and noticed an ad for a store that was closing. Now I'd heard of the store, but not that location. I went there, wandered around for a few minutes and thought there's nothing here for me. Then in the back, tucked away behind some other gaudy pieces, I saw this sofa that was exactly the right size and the unique color I wanted. When I was going to the front to pay for the sofa I saw this beautiful table that they were just taking out of the box. I negotiated for a few minutes and came home with both. I had put the dollar amount for the leather sofa–that was an unusual size and color–on my list at $600 or less and the coffee table at $250 or less. And even though these were seemingly impossible, I decided that was my spending limit. I paid $589 for both pieces, which included delivery. Both pieces would have normally cost $2500 on sale.

A piano

I thought that I would like to have a piano in my living room, but I never did anything to make it happen. The idea bounced around in my head for a while. When I placed baby grand piano on my master list is when things started to happen. I had no idea how this was going to get accomplished. It seemed impossible, out of my budget and just a dream. A few months later I received a call from a friend of mine in the process of divorcing. She had a beautiful black baby grand piano and wanted to find it a temporary home rather than put it into storage. She asked if I would like to baby-sit her baby grand piano for a few months. My first response was "You're kidding" then I immediately said yes. Never mind that I had never played a piano or even considered playing piano. It seemed like a great opportunity to have a beautiful piece of furniture grace my living room, at no cost. So it moved in and I began taking lessons.

I was the loving sitter, and novice player, for this baby grand piano and then a year later it went to it's new home. Because it seemed that my wish had already been fulfilled, I now started my search in earnest for a piano.

I again put it on the master list and put a **very** low $1300 price beside it, even though all the pianos I looked at had been priced at $5,000 to $30,000 or more. It was all my budget could handle and I thought, well let's just see if this is possible. About 2 weeks later I happened to drop a local discount paper on the way to the trash, one I never read before, it opened to the page of musical instruments. The angels sang, the skies opened, and the seas parted and there my piano was listed at a lower price than I wanted. It was delivered a week later and now I'm a concert pianist, in my dreams. Maybe I should put that on the list in earnest.

Rule number 2
—Know How Much
You Want to or Can Spend

How many times have you gone shopping for a specific item only to come home with something that you just settled for? And may I mention you probably paid way too much for it? How many times have you gone out shopping for no particular reason and bought something that you really didn't want or really need? How many times have you bought two of something, just in case you can't find it again? How many times have you bought something that you only liked and didn't absolutely love? How many times have you spent more money than you thought you would—then you find it on sale somewhere else for half the price? How many times have you made that buy that was expensive just because you "gotta have it" only to have buyers remorse about the sticker price?

Every time you make a purchase and bring something home that you are not completely fulfilled and happy with, you are creating an internal dialogue that says, "I will settle for less than exactly what I desire." Every day you think about or see that item, you are *unconsciously* reminded that you paid too much for it. If you wear that item, you make it easier to allow yourself to create the pattern where you will settle for less than you deserve and less than what you wanted. You are reminded that you don't even like the item and because you paid for it, you feel obligated to use it, keep it, or wear it. Each time you see that item you are essentially kicking yourself for buying and/or overpaying for the item. These are some of our unconscious thoughts that happen after we've talked ourselves into purchases that do not meet our true desire.

Sometimes a little more patience is necessary but mostly, this rule is about the clarity you must have around your desired item. The more you understand the amount you want or can spend on something, the more easily it will happen for you within the confines of your budget allotment.

A negative buying situation is where you create a pattern that becomes a habit of making buying decisions and purchases that do not meet your standards. Your standards deserve to be high. You do deserve all that you wish for! It doesn't matter what your standards are, this is about you and what YOU and you alone wish for, not what someone else tells you is best, looks best, or fits their idea of what works for you.

It's your money, no one else is going to get it for you, give it to you, or earn it for you. Well, that is unless you've recently won the lottery, inherited millions or happen to be a teenager today (Note to teenagers: It might be a good idea to use some of these techniques so that you know how to acquire things when the parental gravy train stops). Always know how much you can spend. Always know how much you are willing to spend or part with before the start of **any** shopping/hunting adventure. Having clarity about the amount of money you are willing to part with/spend and referring to your master list will help your mind hold the image easily. Even if you don't have to worry so much about money, having clarity in what you are willing to spend will only help you to find that special item–fast. It is significantly easier to acquire anything you want or need, being specific about the money aspect in order for your success to happen effortlessly. I don't know of one person who wants to be kicked every day, so why should you set yourself up for this unconscious torture? This is like Chinese water torture, so stop and think before you make the purchase.

**A few good questions to keep in mind
when making a purchase:**

Is this <u>exactly</u> what I want to pay
for this item and are these the <u>exact</u>
specifications for this purchase?

Am I settling for something
other than what I truly want?

Does it fit or am I hoping it will fit?

Do I really want this or is my friend
helping me to want this?

Is there enough money in my account
to pay for this today?

There are certain ratio rules that apply to someone when they are purchasing a house. Why should those ratio rules be thrown out the door for general every day purchases? Again, it is a must, to know how much money you are willing to spend on an item. Do not break this rule, because every time you break this rule then you've created what we stated earlier, a negative buying situation. Just because it's shiny, pretty and you like it for the moment, doesn't mean that you need to take it home. STOP! THINK! If you have any hesitation, listen to that loudspeaker in your head that says "PUT THE ITEM DOWN AND LEAVE IMMEDIATELY".

Remember that if you don't know how much you want to spend, the salesperson knows how much they want you to spend. **More**. Spending is a choice not an obligation, as you may have been under the impression. To spend or to spend wisely, that is the question.

Shotgun Shopping

Anecdotes about spending:

I had a special black tie event to attend and was hoping to
make some high-powered connections. This was a business
event and I needed to make a statement that was elegant yet
professional. I knew I only had $175 to spend. I made my list
and realized that I only had one day to find the right dress
It all came together, I got a fabulous dress and made those
critical business connections—all at less than $175.00.

Another time was when I was traveling in London. I knew
it would be cold and wore boots, which happened to have
higher heels. The kind that aren't meant for walking long
distances. I believed I would be walking only 2-3 blocks.
Well, it turned out that I had to walk about half a mile, didn't
know where I was going and couldn't find a taxi. After 3
days of this my feet were screaming. I didn't have the luxury
of enough time and wasn't coming across any shops to find
another pair of shoes. After the event, I was walking through
the airport and just couldn't take the pain one minute longer,
as there was no where to sit while waiting for my flight. I
spotted a shoe shop and all I wanted were shoes that didn't
hurt. I tried on one pair of boots that felt quite comfortable and
bought them. A few stores later I walked into this exquisite
store. I was the only customer, and exhausted, saw empty
comfy chairs and asked to try on a particular pair of boots,
flats. OH MY God they felt amazing and like my feet were
in a cloud. I bought them, paid for them and didn't even look
at the receipt. Well, I knew they would be expensive because
of the exchange rate but I didn't know that they would be the

64

most expensive boots I'd ever purchased. Thank God I truly love them.

What a lesson in "know how much you want to spend" and don't let pain be your guide to making the purchase. Be aware of the exchange rate and take along a comfortable pair of shoes no matter where you're going. Just a side note about these boots: They have become my most adored and most comfortable pair of boots I've ever owned.

A client of mine was telling me that her bedroom is her most sacred place and yet since her divorce, she did nothing to change the look or feel of it. She even had a golf picture that her husband had left hanging above the fireplace. My eyes opened wide and I said, you really need to reclaim that bedroom as yours. I gave her the instructions to have a new picture and a new bedding ensemble in place in less than 30 days. I also gave her the instruction to spend less than $200 on her bedding. She started to object but said she was willing to try. I received an email from her the next week. She had found the most amazing picture she could live with for the rest of her life. Another week or so went by and I received another email. She had also found the most amazing bedding for only $69 that would have cost her retail over $400 and now she absolutely loves her room again.

Rule number 3 —How Much is Your Time Worth?

Have you ever walked around saying things like "I don't have enough time," or "I've got so much on my plate," or "It's too hard to get everything done?" Most people walk around thinking about how little time they have. They repeat the mantra of "I have too much on my plate." They also say, "It's too hard to get everything done." It could be so simple, but our lives have been structured such that time has almost become our enemy. The way we talk about it and how little we seem to have astounds me, because we all have the same amount of time—every day.

If everyone walked around saying the opposite of how little time they have, time might expand. I know this sounds impossible but when things get down to crunch *time,* you often discover your time **is** worth a lot. At crunch time it seems that you are able to accomplish more than ever, yet you still had the same amount of time as before. Why is that? It is because you just have to, no matter what. There are no other options at that point, so time seems to expand to your need.

You can never recapture lost time, but you can save yourself from losing it in the first place. Just so you have clarity and truly understand this rule;

You never lose time, you only let it use you.

One who is a slave to a watch and time is one with a mentality of not having enough—a lack mentality. Each and every one of us has the same amount of time as the other and some know and use the laws of letting time work for them, and the ones that see it with "lack vision" are the ones who are enslaved by time.

Just by saying a simple phrase "I have more than enough time," frequently, through those days that you are stressed and stretched will make things easier. This has worked well for me again and again, as time magically seems to appear. I've had clients and friends try this throughout the years and the outcome seems miraculous. Some have even returned, saying I have so much extra time that I didn't know what to do with myself.

Here's a fun technique to start having time work for you, rather than against you. Allocate a specific amount of time if you are stopping by a store. An example of this is to shop on your way home after you've promised to be home at a certain time. But if you use this trick ensure that you stick to the items on your list. Another good opportunity is when you find yourself with an extra minute or three, go into that new store that you've wanted to check out and scan the area. By scanning, I mean just do a quick walk through and look but don't pick anything up. This is a honed skill, but one that gets more efficient with repeated use. This way you've scoped the layout and have a general idea if you want to return to that store. You could find out that the store has the wrong styles for your lifestyle and you will have saved a great deal of time later.

The best thing I ever did with buying excursions was to be on a time budget. Because I can't stand to shop, somehow giving myself a short time line to go in to a store, translated into the fact that I wasn't really shopping. Also, because I give thought to what I need, keeping that list in mind or in my wallet, with specifics, I am then able to breeze through a store, quickly identifying what to buy or what not to buy.

Refuse to allow the "not enough time" beast to take possession of you, just because you seem to feel squeezed for every second. Breathe and get back to the mantra "I have more than enough time". You make your own time machine and can stretch time by selecting how you use it, how you view it and what you say about it. Breathing actually expands time. Holding our breath actually uses more time and resources making us unfocused and feeling more pressed than usual.

Why is determining what your time is worth necessary? Because if you don't then you'll end up feeling like everyone is pushing and pulling on you. It becomes their time and not yours. You are a slave to the worry about time. So, by knowing how much your time is worth, means that you have a different attitude towards the push/pull. You will find that you may even be able to say no to things that someone else can or should handle. You may discover, like I have, that maybe it just doesn't need to get done right this minute.

Let's say that you're a mom and your spouse/partner earns $75,000 per year. How does that translate into dollars for you? Your income is a portion, should be half of that because of what you accomplish each day with your children. I'm sure there will be a lot of argument about this one, but at least you will have a different point of view about the value of time. Begin to realize that each "gotta do" or "gotta have" on your list is essential or else it needs to be removed from the list. You want to consider and then remember that your time is valuable. Whether you are shopping or not you need to know how much your time is worth. You will find that shopping becomes more efficient when you know that you are worth say $50 per hour, and that hour can be used for more essential activities such as spending time with your family, taking care of something that has been nagging you as well as eating mental energy and space, etc.

Your time is worth a lot and how you choose to use it is one of those priceless things. By choosing to use it differently, you will have more ease and internal peace. Giving yourself permission to use time the way you choose, can relieve you of stress and allow joy.

Remember the adage—Give something that needs to get done to someone who is busy, because it will easily get done! Somehow those who view time as just that "time" seem to be able to accomplish more in the time given. Give yourself permission, right now, to make time your friend. Use it differently and see what wonderfulness comes from that.

Take this moment in time and BREATHE.

Ah – that feels so wonderful.

Stories about time:

One day I was procrastinating as I didn't want to attend an event that was a two hour drive away. It was something I had committed to without thinking and had to pay for beforehand and was stressed about the whole event and the money. I raced to get in my car and on the road, had about one and a half hours to make the two hour drive. The entire time, with the radio turned off, I repeated "It's ok I'm already there" again and again and again. I turned onto the street where I was to park and meet the group and had about 5 minutes before we had to leave on the bus. I truly collapsed time.

I have so many of these stories and one where we had a 15 hour drive that truly only took us 11 hours. To this day I cannot tell you the specifics of how that happened, other than we used yogic breathing and aligned our thoughts to the need of getting there in the shortest amount of time.

Rule number 4 —Follow Your Instincts (TRUST)

As I mentioned earlier this is an important rule because this is where you'll do the best manifesting, stretch yourself a bit, and have some of the most fun with your non-shopping ventures. After you get over the need to control and be dictated to by old unconscious habits, you will have a lot of fun and enjoyment in your buying choices. You may even have some of your own stories to tell. Once you allow this piece (TRUST) into your life, with seeking items and with making your purchases, you will find yourself applying these techniques in other areas. Always follow your instinct and go where you feel you should go, even if it's not a place you are sure about. OK OK here's the disclaimer—be safe.

Instincts get honed over the years and after a few bad decisions somehow we get down on ourselves about ones from the past that went wrong. Our instinctual self—gets smaller and smaller and often gets pushed so far to the back that we forget we can have good instincts. Often we operate from skepticism, because we've had a so-called bad experience, making us refrain from truly hearing and acting on our instincts. Fear is another aspect of how we operate. We stop following our instincts because we're afraid it will turn out wrong or badly. What about all the decisions that went right, because you followed your instinct?

Once you recapture the habit of listening to your "gut" or instinct you will discover it only becomes easier. You may need to experiment in the beginning as sometimes when it seemed like instinct, it was really your head tripping you up, getting in the way. We need to stop and hear, not just listen, to **our quietest inner voice** that persists about something— this is instinct and an aspect of your higher self.

Another simple technique is to STOP saying you have bad instincts! We all make choices and decisions, some great some not so great, but no matter what, you still have instincts and good ones, otherwise we wouldn't be able to survive day to day. It's just a matter of choosing to pay attention to our inner voice and follow those instincts. It's our "free will" that can cause one action or a contrary action. When we start telling ourselves that we make good choices, all of a sudden we begin to make better choices. We are a product of what we tell ourselves. We are also a product of how well we listen to ourselves.

Paying attention to your body and its signals when using instinct is very beneficial. For example, if your stomach is feeling tight about an item or place then maybe it's your quietest self telling you something is not right. If you feel somewhat nauseous about a particular decision, then your body may be telling you the situation is not ok—or you could just be hungry. Conversely, you might find your stomach feeling like it's full of little butterflies, which is just nervous tension and usually that means you are on the right track—but may be the venturing into waters that are new and exciting. There could be some discomfort with a new venture but you will feel joyous for having gone through such an event.

There are some obvious inner voices that are a good idea to refrain from following. These include knowing that you are at your spending limit but deciding you are going to buy the item anyway, no matter the consequence. Another is that you won't be able to pay for what you are about to purchase, except with another loan on your house. You won't be able to pay for the item over the next credit card statement or at the maximum three months of statements. Unless it's a home and, we know what that means, given the state of the lending industry right now, ensure that you have the right payment and the right loan amount, as a ratio to what you earn.

We don't need glasses for hindsight and we don't need glasses to follow our gut. If your gut is signaling that you should not buy that house even if it seems like it's the best deal on the planet, then you should follow your gut and run to your car. Where we get into the most trouble is through our desires for unrealistic ways of living or showing how we live. This clouds our ability to follow our own instinct. When you follow what seems to be the path of least resistance and allow others to push you to make a decision they want, rather than make our own decision that is right for you, it is likely you will find a great deal of difficulty. When we are being greedy and know this unconsciously, there's a penalty, later.

Check in with your body and if there is discomfort in any area, then make another choice or even better, run for the door. If your body is talking to you in a negative way and you ignore the signals then you'll be taking an antacid later.

You are like a hunting dog, I mean god. Follow your instincts, follow your intuition and allow them to lead you to the right decision. Muster up some courage and move forward while taking action based on your intuition.

Just so you have a memory of how following your instincts works, remember when you were in need of a gift for someone and only thought about giving one item, later finding out that you passed on that item and the gift you chose, had already been given by someone else. Remember a time when you decided on a course of action, followed your instincts and felt joyous about the outcome because it was so on the mark. Remember a time when you took a different route than usual and found out later that there was a traffic jam on the original route. Think about all the times when your instincts were right on target. Each time you recall a situation where you were right and eliminate the times when it wasn't just right is like giving your brain traction to make positive actions day in and day out.

Stories about instinct:

While traveling in India I had lost our big book that was to give us maps and details about where to go when traveling. All I had left was a small piece of paper that gave us some city names and a general idea of what order to visit each city. I had made a reservation with a travel agent of a local friend and trusted that that agent would get us to where we needed. Turns out we missed our first flight and thus missed the travel agent, who was to meet us at the airport. We were on our own, no map, no guide and just a small piece of paper that contained the general idea of where we wanted to go.

Everything was working out in our favor it seemed, in every aspect of our trip. Then we got to an area where they did not speak much English. We hired a driver that would take us to the cities we wished to travel to. His favorite phrase when trying to decide which way to go—was "Miss I have doubt." This came about as we would tell him we wanted to go to a particular place and he would ask directions. After asking directions he would get to a place in the general area and then tell us he had doubt. My retort was always – "No Doubt, erase, erase. It's ok, NO doubt." Well it seemed that time and again we got to the places that we wanted to go with little resistance.

I didn't know until I returned to the U.S. and talked with some friends, who grew up in India, some of the places we chose to go to, took most people weeks of travel time to get to, visit and then get out of. All I knew is that I had a certain amount of time and needed to get back on a particular day. I knew that I wanted to go to specific places and see specific sites. To this day, it is a cherished story among client's and friends. It demonstrates all the rules—List, How Much to Spend, in Time and Money, using Instinct and a great deal of TRUST.

When my dad told me about a stock that I should buy I decided to buy it even though it didn't feel right. I listened to his enthusiasm about where the company was headed and what was being done in the industry. Fortunately, I only bought a small number of shares but I didn't listen to my gut, which said NO this doesn't work for you. The stock now has lost a lot of value and I lost money.

I have one client who buys things because she's feeling that high from the moment. Sales people see her coming. Every time she hears her inner voice, telling her not to make the purchase, she goes against this inner voice and is bedridden for 2 days. After reading the manuscript for this book, she's now following her instincts better.

Rule number 5
—Don't Get the Salesperson Involved

This rule is a little tricky because you may want help in some situations, yet in others it is in your best interest to have limited interaction with a sales person. The general idea behind this rule is that by now you will know what you want and the specifics of time and money involved. That's really the best time to involve a sales person.

If you are still unsure or just "browsing" then do not engage their assistance. They will take up your precious time and can sway you into considering something that's neon when you were going for pastel. Also remember that they have a job and it is their job to sell you something.

A salesperson can be helpful if you're in the fact finding or hunting phase of shopping, and you have a lot of time to spare. This is where you'll have to have the frame of mind, that you need only a specific amount of information within a specific amount of time, and the salesperson is the key to the information. If the salesperson is going off on their own

tangent and you've got to go, then back away and divert your attention to something else to break the link. This will ensure that your time is yours and not the salesperson's.

If a salesperson is rude to you, then obviously this is not the right shop to buy from or the right person to help you. Sometimes they are just plain pushy, that's another time when you want to remove yourself from that store or environment. Should the salesperson have an offensive attitude that isn't

working for you then that's the time to move along.

The more certainty you have in and around you the more the salesperson is likely to leave you to your browsing. When you have a timid look or air about you is when a salesperson usually takes the reigns and guides you to a product that may not be exactly what you had in mind.

Because at one time in my life I was a salesperson, I wanted to give the client the information and empower them to make the decision, rather than to sell them on the product. Selling a product like this felt more authentic to me. When you encounter sales people who are authentic you will feel well cared for and empowered, conversely you will know when you are being sold something. The more authentic someone is the more easy the buying interaction. This is one of those instinctual things we just know.

Stories about salesperson help

Recently I was in need of a specific type of outfit for an event and had some colors in mind. I was in the changing room and overheard this salesperson, who was not on commission, gushing to a customer how wonderful each item looked on her. Because it was so loud I decided to look out and see what the woman was trying on To my surprise only about half of the items looked like she should be wearing them. I thought wow this person is out of sync with the inauthenticity of the salesperson.

I was with a friend who was trying on a particularly expensive coat with the store owner helping us. While the store owner was authentic about his love for the product, what became obvious was that he had a vested interest in selling the coat. He was telling us that the short-sleeve length was in style. Now really, a slightly too short sleeve is very uncomfortable and definitely not what looked good on my friend. So the salesperson was helpful only to a point, his interest in selling the coat being greater than the reality of what was comfortable for my friend. We left, without buying the coat.

The other day I was in a store and truly wanted help. The salesperson took ignoring me to the extreme. She was too busy on her cell phone to discuss price and my question about other sizes, to care whether I really wanted to buy something or not. I actually wanted a men's shirt but I left the store promptly and stood outside deciding where to cross the street. I noticed a For Sale sign in the store window. Obviously there was something going on with that salesperson and her attitude. She had no vested interest in helping me and the sign just validated what I felt. Hmmm how interesting.

My dad told me he and his wife were in the market for a new car. The first place they went the salesman was rude and basically unwilling to help. They decided to drive to a more distant dealer, finding a salesman that my dad said was annoying at first, as he didn't seem fast enough. After making the purchase from this particular salesman, he reflected on the entire process and thought the salesman had so much class and taste, wanting to ensure they were cared for. It wasn't that he was slow, it was his nature to go the extra mile. It turned out this was the dealers top salesman.

Rule number 6
—Do Not Shop With the
"Shop-a-holic" Type

D on't go shopping with friends who love to shop or who shop all the time. Don't shop with people who love to stop at every single item, touch it and caress it. Don't go shopping with those who must go into every single store. You will be miserable. If they want to go shopping and have lunch, then meet them for lunch but never, or almost never, go shopping with the "shop-a-holic." The shop-a-holic will just look at every — single rack and try on a hundred items even though you already know it won't work for them. This type of person will want to pick everything up and tell YOU about how great it would be for YOU. By having one of these types help you with styles or colors or flavors you will need to stay strong in your convictions as to what you like and do not like, what style works for you. You will need to be strong and clear about how much you can spend, if you shop with these types. NO must be a word used often in these situations. Or you could just divert and change the subject, tell them how good some item would be for them.

By now if you *are* the non-shopper on a shopping excursion with a "shop-a-holic" type, then you will be fantasizing about your escape. You will find ways to check messages, text someone, visit other stores or sections of the store while your friend continues to shop. You will sneak or want to sneak and go get something to eat — anything but endure another minute of the minutia. It's likely that you've said a number of times "Ok let's go now".

Shop-a-holic types or those who really love to shop, have out of body experiences. Their eyes glaze over and they become blank to hearing anything. The best time to shop with a shop-a-holic is when you don't know the area, when you need a specific type of style, or when you really need to get out of your own head.

The shop-a-holic type of person is dangerous because you can get talked into or hooked into their needs and their wants. Then you will end up purchasing something that is just not right for you. If you have clarity about what you want and someone else intervenes or interferes you may just as well plan on going to the store twice. Once when you're there with your friend and once when you have to go back and return the item.

Stories about shopping with mom, the shopper of all shoppers

Once, when my mother was visiting me and I wanted to give her some joy I hooked her up with a friend of mine to go to the local swap meet. Now you can imagine that this would not be a place that I would want to go and so I was happily going to spend the day catching up on some home projects. Of course, that is until I got the guilt from my mother about how short her visit would be and how nice it would be to spend the day together, outside. I thought, ok how bad could it be, if I'm outside. The three of us went and they had to stop at every single booth. We were there for more than 4 hours. At least they had a blast. This was the last time I went shopping like that with my mother.

Another time my mother was visiting during Christmas and I needed to get one additional item as a gift for the party we were to attend. I told her I was going to the mall to go to one specific store and my mother's eyes lit up, next thing you know she was going with me. Fortunately, I prevailed and we went to one store, bought the item, then promptly left for a total visit of about 15 minutes. I was happy, but my mother was aghast at how I could go to the mall and not go into another store while there. Her question to me as we briskly walked out the door was,

"Aren't we going anywhere else?"

I was with some friends and had stayed in Chicago after a business trip to do some Christmas shopping. They had a number of stores they "needed" to go to. One of them was this multi-story store for kids, which shall remain nameless. It sounded like a good idea, actually sounded fun until I felt like we had been there most of the day. Turned out we had really only been in there about 40 minutes by then. She had something specific in mind that only this store carried. We

had to go to each floor in search of the item because somehow a salesperson never materialized. Needless to say she never found the item and we were 2 hours late for our lunch date.

Rule number 7
—Decree That You Will
Not Need to Return Things

Notice that I didn't say commit or decide, I said decree that you will not return things. A lot of people have a fear of making big commitments and shopping can be about committing to the right acquisition. Shopping can be daunting because it requires decisions and "Shotgun Shopping" is about getting to the heart of quick decisions, right choices and great deals. So if you just decree, set firmly in place the thought that you will not need to return items, you will find yourself with what you need and ultimately not need to return anything. This rule allows your brain to stay focused and achieve maximum results quickly.

I had an unsaid and unwritten rule that was a secret, even to me. That is until recently. The rule was, never return anything. It was secret because I always seemed certain about what I bought and if I didn't' love it I didn't buy it. If it wasn't in my budget then I found a way to earn extra income to buy it or I didn't buy it at all. Little did I know that I had saved a lot of time and headache making certain and clear decisions so as to not return anything.

Several years ago I bought a pair of shoes that felt great in the store, but found out later they absolutely hurt my feet when I walked. I tried to endure but just couldn't handle them. I even wore them a few more times and got cuts on my feet. So I, for the first time that I could recall, had to face returning them or never wearing them again. I decided to return them and that I wanted the money back. It was a strange sensation that I was having difficulty with this and found that I felt shame about having to return something. Almost as if making a mistake was going to get me into trouble which made me consider keeping them. I even wore them a few more times after the cuts and got blisters, just to be sure that I had made a mistake.

That's when I began talking with friends about the idea of having to return something for the first time, and found that people return things all the time. This was such a novel idea to me that I had to seriously review what it was, that made me so clear about making purchases. Why had I not needed to return something until then? What was my thinking and what were my actions that up until that point, kept me from having to return anything? When you purchase something that doesn't fit or isn't right for you, then you end up having to return the item, or just keeping it to avoid all the behind the scenes emotions. At that point it became clear to me that shopping was so distasteful that it was imperative to only go once, and positively not need to return.

I heard a story about the purchase and wearing of a cute pair of shoes that applies to this "need to not return anything" rule. A friend had on a really cute pair of shoes and I commented that I liked them. She then tells me that for months after she bought them every part of where the shoe hit had a blister. She kept them because she didn't want to return them, as they were too cute and she said she would endure the pain to ensure that she didn't have to return them. She told me that they are *now, after a few months and some scars*, pretty comfortable. Wow, I thought, what torture you put your body through, just so you kept these cute shoes.

Returning things in a busy world and busy life creates more overall consumption. It creates more stress, takes up space and time in our physical lives and our brains, that we could use for other wonderful encounters in our lives. Having to return an item makes us consume more gas and more overall energy. It ties up our precious resources, and keeps us from attaining our true desire.

Let me just say that it's not a bad idea to return things that aren't right for you, but many people just keep the item and don't deal or want to deal with returns. Just so you know, there are a lot of emotions about returns that tap into "not good enough" and "have to be perfect" and "shame about not getting it right the first time". These types of emotions can help people keep things that are not right for them. Some, even wear things that they know are not right for them. I know of women and men who have items in their closets and garages that have not been used because they've convinced themselves that they will use them in the future.

I think of these things that are sitting around for future use taking space in our brains and lives. It also reminds me of making a purchase that has a rebate and you have to go through hoops to save $2. You've driven across town to save $2 and then you forget to claim the rebate money.

There are many return policies that apply to large and small stores but just the fact that you are aware of the return policy should help you make more precise decisions. Since that first time of taking those shoes back I have made a few returns but I still adhere to the overall rule of the right item at the right price. I have even taken food back to the market that was bad or tasted bad.

Again, having clarity around **your** needs, **your** likes, **your** dislikes, and **your** willingness to let go of something because it doesn't suit you, will decrease the need to return items. By having the ability to say no to something that isn't right for you in the first place, will only result in having the right item in the first place. This type of clarity will improve your decision-making and can be applied to any situation.

Return if you must, but I challenge you to use the techniques here so that you don't have to return things and that you make the right purchase or acquisition the first time around. You deserve the best the first time around, even if it takes a little longer to get it.

Stories about keeping things that aren't right for you:
I have a friend who told me recently that she has an old desk in the house she's lived in for 10 years, from the previous owner. She has always thought the desk to have negative energy but her reasoning for keeping it was that it fits in that spot, perfectly. She felt bad about having the space empty and didn't want to say no to the seller who was so willing to give it up. Now she's never liked it, has felt negative energy towards it, and on top of all of that it reminds her that the woman who owned the piece before, died from cancer. Oh and one piece that is important to mention is that my friend has battled with cancer and feels there's some connection. I would say this is one of those situations when it's time to send it to the recycler or use it as firewood.

I was recently told about a painting my friend has in her family room that her mother insisted she have. Her mother also insisted that she hang the painting in the focal point of her family room. She truly ha_es this painting and the imagery behind it. Every time she walks into that room, she said it makes her feel depressed and sad and yet she put it up because of her mother's insistence. She didn't want to say no because she was afraid to have it go to her brother. The painting is worth a lot of money and rather than let it go and allow good things to come as a result of letting it go, she's holding on and doesn't like to spend time inside her home. It's a picture that her brother would enjoy but she elects to keep it to keep supposed peace.

This story is a twist on how to ensure that you get the right size, the right color, and style. I wanted a pair of white sandals and hadn't been able to find any, so I decided to shop for shoes, for the first time, on-line. While I was making my selection I thought it would be a smart idea to buy a few different pairs. I decided that I didn't want to go through any returns or the risk that I would get the wrong size. So I order 3 pairs in 3 sizes and had them shipped. The prices were so reasonable that the idea of paying for return shipping was worth it. I received this large box, my boyfriend raised his eyebrows and laughed, then helped me decide which pair to keep. Putting the rest back in the box, taping it and placing it outside for pick up, I ended up with one fantastic pair of sandals, at a great price, in the right size.

Rule number 8
—Know the details
—Before leaving the house

Really, "Shotgun Shopping" is about obtaining what you desire, without spending too much time, money or aggravation. Buying or finding things that are right the first time certainly makes life easier. You will have more time when you buy the right item the first time around and you'll be much more proud of yourself.

There is one caveat that is important to note here. Waiting until the absolute perfect time or when the stars, moon and sun are in perfect alignment means that you may have passed up your heart's desire. So remember to take a bit of courage and buy it when the time is ripe.

Beside each item, in addition to the amount to spend, that I identify on my list are some notes (always leave just enough space for brief notes). The notes could be the size of the item, it could be the dimensions, it could be as simple as the color you wish the item to be. The notes could be about where you saw it advertised, or it could be when you need to get that item. A note could also be when you expect or need to make the purchase. If you make a note about when you expect the item to come to you please write the words "or sooner." See the example box.

When it comes to this rule, you may think, duh. But, how many times have you gone shopping for an item just to get an idea, think that you found exactly what you need, only to realize that you don't have the measurements or have certainty about the color? You then have to make another trip. I say, who really has time for this? The reason for this rule is that you really want to have as much information at your fingertips, so that when you think you've found the right item, it truly has all the right qualities. I have even gone so far as to staple a picture of the color and a swatch of fabric to the list.

Example:	
Manolo Blanick, shoes	$125 or less Size 7, pink
Leather sofa	$600 or less, 42" goldtone
Camera-digital	$459 or less, T-shot
	12/12/09 or sooner

This is such a simple rule that requires only a little preparation beforehand, that there's not much else to be said about it other than just do it.

NOTE: Along with knowing the details it is important to remember to actually take this precious list with you. I say this knowing how many times I've forgotten my list.

Story about knowing what you want:

There's a story about a local realtor who met up with a new client. The client turned out to be the ideal client. Had lots of money. Wanted a large house and was willing to pay cash. It was all ideal except for one thing, the client looked at hundreds of homes and was in the almost going to write an offer category several times, but he just couldn't seem to find the "perfect" house. There seemed to always be some flaw that prevented the deal from happening. Six years later he's still living in an apartment and the market is ripe and the house he saw that he just loved and had no flaws is not available. Know what you want and be willing to take the step to make that happen.

Best Times to Avoid Any Shopping —Period!

Avoid the store:

If the store smells funny turn around and leave promptly. The last thing in the world you need is to have to endure weird smells while you're shopping. A weird smell could definitely mean that you make an impulse buy that turns into one of those negative buying situations.

I walked into a store the other day and barely got a foot inside, with my hand still on the door, the smell was so odd that I turned around and went directly back to my car. There was another time when I walked into a bath and beauty store, and the smells were so conflicting and overpowering, that I had to put my hand over my nose to make my purchase. This is one time when I found a salesperson and told her what I needed, promptly made the purchase and raced out of the store.

Avoid the store:

When the music conflicts with how you wish to feel or is something that is offensive. I really wanted to go into a particular store one day and got about 2 steps inside and realized the music was making me feel irritated. I decided to try to continue, made it 10 steps in, touched a few items and then just left. Took a big breath and thought, what a shame that I probably would not go back to that store again.

Avoid the store:

When the clerk is angry or storming around. This situation means that you should find another clerk or just leave the store. Just because the clerk is having a bad day, due to who knows what, doesn't mean that you should subject yourself to acquiring their bad day vibes. Interacting with someone else who is having a bad day can infect your good day.

Of course there's another philosophy I have around this, which is to see how quickly I can get the clerk to crack a smile. I usually say something to compliment someone, and next thing you know they are much less grumpy.

Avoid the store:

This one may not apply to you, but as I cannot stand **crowds of people,** trying to buy the same thing or that frenzy around fire sales, basement sales, after Christmas sales, etc. I've found that I avoid those, completely. I work to acquire what I want through clarity of the end result, along with the amount I'm willing to spend, "Shotgun Shopping". Use these techniques, so you don't go home all frustrated for not getting that special item, because Sally Shopper stole it out from under you.

Not to mention that when you're in line and possibly a long line, you have to listen to people grumbling about how long it's taking and how long it's going to take and how they need to get home. Grumbling and listening to people grumble or complain is a big drain on your energy.

Avoid the store:

If the **lines are too long** or 20 deep and you have limited time. Many people are addicted to their brand of coffee or latte and will wait in long lines to get their fix. I say find the ideal time and avoid the line, rather than get frustrated. That type of frustration will carry through the rest of the day if you're not careful.

Avoid the store:

One should not shop **when they are feeling irritated**. If you absolutely must shop when irritated, then go with the attitude that you will plaster a smile on your face so that you don't share your gloom and irritation with others. Some may say they are irritated all the time but for that I say take a few deep breaths, given that you've probably been holding it and not truly breathed for hours. See what good you can share through your time of irritation. If you give yourself a few sighs and deep breaths you will be much more prepared to interact with people than if irritated. Or you could just feel light headed and out of breath which is certainly better than irritation.

Avoid the store:

If you are feeling hungry or have to go to the bathroom too badly. These are optimal times when you will make decisions just to get the item and get it over with. Then you'll end up having to return it and start all over again.

Avoid the store:

When it's **stifling hot** during the summer and there's no A/C. You'll make poor decisions when in a store such as this. Here in the U.S. you may not find this situation very often. If you really need to be in a store at such a time then stick to the rules, make your purchase and graciously exit saying thank you. Be grateful that your car has air conditioning and turn the air on full.

Avoid the store:

If you hear people in the store arguing, leave. Another sign that you shouldn't be in that store. I was once on the ski slopes, lost my gloves and needed to buy a new pair. I stopped by a local shop, intent on finding gloves and did not pay too much attention to my surroundings when I walked in. There was a man standing at the counter yelling at the clerk about how expensive everything was and accusing the clerk of numerous things. I had found the gloves but I didn't leave and stood behind the yelling customer saying quietly under my breath it's ok just be nice, be nice, be nice (repeatedly) and all of a sudden the wife came to the counter and whisked the angry husband away. I promptly left the store and bought my gloves somewhere else.

Avoid the store:
When it's too cluttered to move around easily. When this is going on in a store your energy gets compressed. When your energy is compressed you feel pressured to buy something and buy it fast.

When traveling to other countries that don't have the space that we have, this rule may not apply. You may find some amazing item in the corner, hiding.

Avoid the store:
While feeling down or depressed, it is not the time to shop. It will only create another negative buying situation. You will buy something, take it home and it will remind you of when you weren't in the best place, space or frame of mind.

Avoid the store:

If the salesperson ignores you when you are in need of making that special purchase. Why in the world would you want to shop there? I learned this early in my non-shopping years when I had to buy a gown for a formal dinner. When I walked in, the salesperson first ignored me and then when I did get help from another salesperson she insulted me by saying that I wouldn't be able to afford the dresses I was sorting through. Next, the same clerk insulted me by telling me my size, which happened to be four sizes too large.

If you cannot avoid any of these difficult situations, I suggest you limit your time in such stores. This of course can almost go without being said, but I know of several people who have stayed in a store and complained the entire time about the service, price, and wait, just because they liked the brand.

If you think about the energy surrounding such a purchase from a negative situation then you could possibly have a negative interaction when wearing the clothes or when you see the item you've purchased. Know that your brain stores every situation. Even if you don't recall every single situation, they are all stored in your unconscious and your mood may react to those negative energies.

Additional avoidance note:

Shopping on the television is not considered "Shotgun Shopping." It may be a good place to get information and get clear about what you want but those programs are designed to take you through an emotional buy. Also, there is a pressure to take action in their time frame. So window shopping through the television is OK, but making an impulse buy because it sounds like an amazing deal is truly not in your best interest.

Best Times to Shop; No, Really, THE Best Times to Shop

Of course many people will say the best time to shop is when you feel like it, but for the "Shotgun Shopper" we need a little adjustment on the best times to shop.

When the weather turns for the first time and it's raining or snowing, most people want to stay at home and hibernate. Not me, I realized years ago it is easier to go out there in these conditions because the streets are virtually empty and the stores are empty of the hordes of people. You actually get people who are pleasant and if you want help, you get people who want to help you during these times. So I actually relish the change in weather for the mere pleasure of no harassment and good connections with the people in the stores. This also applies to the first warm days but you need to time it just right to miss traffic.

First thing in the morning right after the store has opened and right before lunch are great times to shop. You've got the place to yourself and can even contemplate a few minutes about what you've put on your list for purchase, and how best to acquire it. Another time is when the store is open later than usual, during peak "shopping" times of the year.

Another great day to head out is Super Bowl Sunday. Sorry guys but this is truly a wonderfully quiet time to shop. How about the last 2 hours the store is open before the clocks are changed? Also think about where you live and what events get most people out and in attendance and that's when you'll find it's the best time to shop.

115

Ok now some of you may get mad at me for this one but it really works. **On Sunday** the shopping areas are not usually filled first thing because everyone goes to church. Or at least they say they are at church. So if you really need something and don't want to fight the crowds, go first thing on Sunday morning, before everyone gets out of church and then you can attend a later service.

Another good time to shop is when you have listened to your intuition. If I listen to my intuition about picking something up or driving somewhere, even though it would seem the odds are impossible that it would be anything less than crowded, I find that there are fewer people around and things move much more quickly. You can prove this theory out just by the fact that at some point you have said, now is a good time to get in line and you have all you need, but you continue to browse and next thing you know the lines are packed. You might want to go back to review the **Trust Rule**.

Remember, the other times good for shopping for many experienced "Shotgun Shoppers" is **when there's not a minute to waste.** It will seem that many follow this rule during the holidays and wait till the last minute, but this is not what I mean by "Shotgun Shopping." Although this may work for some, it usually puts pressure on the gift purchaser and those on the road. If you are on your way somewhere and have just got to get that item then apply the rules, see how much fun you can have with finding just the right item.

The other day I was in need of getting a gift for someone I met only once for an exchange and had limited information. I stood in the middle of the store and thought "Ok, **I am guided to the right item for this person**," whose name I couldn't even remember but whose face was clear in my mind. I repeated this and found a wonderful blouse nearly alone on a rack. It turned out to be just what she needed. I have found more wonderful gifts through this simple practice than I can recount.

Of course there's always the internet and the best time to shop on the internet is when you have the time. This way you'll never have to wait in line. The only thing you have to wait for is how fast the page loads. But boy do you really need to know what you want, the size, the color, and will have to have planned ahead. The internet is NON-shopper's paradise. You will want to ensure that you have the "Shotgun Shopper" rules handy. You will want to know which stores to buy from or else you're defeating the purpose and spending much more time in the hunting phase than is necessary.

Mall Shopping

As you have learned by now, malls are not my favorite places to spend time. Fact is, I avoid malls as often as possible. The only time I like a mall is when it's just about empty of shoppers and there's plenty of parking. Of course that's not something that happens very often. Now don't get me wrong, I love people and spend a great deal of my time with people and in front of large groups of people, but malls and the bad behavior that people seem to acquire once they step into a mall is an experience I just don't want. It seems that something happens to humans when there are too many people in a mall. People seem to forget any manners and have that glazed look in their eyes and will bump into you and step on your feet just to get to where they need to go.

Before you judge, remember that feeling of getting swept up in other people's energy and emotions, hurrying when you're not in a hurry or getting upset when there's no reason in the world to do so. This can and does happen more easily when in the mall, shopping. The best word describing that energy is "frenetic" (excessively agitated, wildly active) and it permeates the walls of most malls. Malls also seem to capture you while time seems to disappear. Before you know it, when you're in a mall environment, you've spent hours there, rather than what was intended originally to be only an hour.

People in other parts of the country make fun of Californians for the outdoor malls, the mini malls, and the malls without walls. I've refined the mall experience and now you'll benefit from this anti mall experience. There are even a few malls in California called the Anti Mall—what a concept. It's premise is to bring people together in an environment that is conducive to calm and sane shopping, giving people the ability to hang out and relax.

Now if it's a holiday, go early or go late to the malls but stay away in between. I thought that malls would be less populated and difficult once internet shopping took off but that seems not to be the case. It seems that they are just as crowded as before, maybe even more so, thus you'll want to ensure that you've got your list and get out the door quickly.

Of late, the large stores seem to have sales that last beyond the normal mall hours. Although this is a recent discovery of mine and this could have been going on for years. It means that you can actually go to a larger store, when most of the world is unaware that the store is open, finding what you want easily. You might actually get out with less hassle than during the normal business hours.

Tips For a Great End to Your Non-Shopping Adventure!

Find the check out counter with the fewest customers. Often times this will be in the men's section or the cosmetic counter. Hah, you say that is impossible. Well if you scan all of them and decide on the one where the people are most relaxed, along with the clerk who seems most calm, you usually get waited on faster. You also want to look for the clerk that's bored, just hanging out shuffling things around and ask her if she can help you at a vacant register. Another tip, which is going to put me on the edge of your minds as very very strange, is to stand in line giving thanks and gratitude that another check stand opens up promptly. The point is, why waste your time in line when you could be out doing something much more productive.

I've actually stood in line at the post office many times when there's a long line or it's a holiday, I repeatedly say "Thank You, thank you, thank you …" or "So happy, so grateful…" or something that shares loving kindness—based on the principles of energy that, the more you give "good," the more you receive "good." Just remember, that there needs to be no doubt while you are doing this. So put your cell phone on silent and try this one.

Just like they say on the phone when you are ordering something or you need to use your credit card for purchase – have your form of payment ready (or near ready). Fumbling in your purse or your pocket for your credit card or cash is a drag on your time and energy. This is so that you get out of there with the least hassle and the shortest amount of time.

Recap

Leave emotion at the door

Identify what YOU like

Know what you need and the specifications

Trust your instincts about an item or store

Buy only what you need

If you feel hesitation about the item run for the door

Buy only what YOU like

Be happy and grateful

Pass along the good to another

Remember, the universe is on your side

Remember, it's easier than you have been telling yourself

Of course you'll want to take out the list that you've created using the tips from this book so that you will have the most amazing experience in manifesting and materializing. All of this is easy. It is something that you do every day. So now allow your brain and life to enjoy the idea that you can manifest or materialize anything easily. You can even materialize things that are not on the good "list." I've changed what Henry Ford said, slightly, "If you think you can't then you can't and if you think you won't find something, then you won't find something. The can't and won't and clutter categories keep you stuck and from attaining what you desire.

So think that you can and you will!

Say that it's possible and it will be so!

Rinse and Repeat!!!

Shopping Karma

You've heard about parking karma, now I'm going to teach you how to increase your karma bank account for shopping. Every time you buy something new you must give two things away. I can hear it now but but but.. Believe me this is the methodology behind *always* finding just the right item at just the right time, from just the right place, at just the right price. Particularly in crunch time. It's as if the universe is saying you gave, now there's a void or space and so now I can provide and fill it more easily.

Every time you create a space, universal law is designed to fill that space. Each time you touch something in your closet that hasn't been worn in a long time or you think "Oh I never liked this" is the perfect time to put it in the give away pile. How many coats or sweaters do you have that you haven't worn in a long long time? Many people organize their space so that they can see everything. The reason for this philosophy is that if they don't see it then they don't remember it's there, so they just accumulate more stuff. Go to the bottom of a desk, or drawer, or back of the closet, or even go to the bottom of a box in the garage and see if you really need every single item that's been stored there. Just allowing space to happen has so much mystery, fun, and a joyous outcome, if you have the desire to experiment.

Two things given away can mean shoes, socks and undergarments, a necklace you have never liked, kitchen appliances that you no longer like or will use, etc. Give that old computer away that's sitting unused on the closet shelf.

I just heard that Costco, of all places, has a program for computers and components that are no longer wanted.

Give the books that you aren't going to read again or refer to again to a school or library, so someone else gets the benefit of the information. The trick is to give away a few things on a regular basis to keep your environment clear of clutter. Clutter is the demon of good shopping karma, because it eats away the good. The more clutter you have, the less flow there is in your day, work, relationships, finances, life, etc. When you get into the flow of giving, it feels fantastic and frees up space in your brain, as well as your life.

There's a lot to be said for the Zen approach – less is more. When you have less, you actually have more. My mother always said that it would be better to have one really good (expensive, sometimes) pair of shoes so that you can be comfortable, walk and have good feet for when you are older, than it is to have a dozen pair of cheap shoes that pinch after 15 minutes. Another rationale for less is more is that the more you have the less time you have, because you will have to spend more time taking care of what you already have. There's an old saying that those who have a cow have to take care of that cow and those that have many cows spend more time taking care of many cows.

Karma is the golden rule of "give and you shall receive." There has to be a general precept of giving and receiving otherwise the universe creates the opportunity to correct the imbalance, sometimes in the most unlikely ways. Only giving or only receiving is like having a clogged spigot that isn't allowing water to flow. It is important, if you are already giving, that you allow yourself to receive. People want balance in their lives but often have not looked at the energetic implications of giving without receiving. When more balance is there, then the journey through life won't have as many bumps.

Oh and just in case you need parking karma for your non-shopping excursions, put extra money in the meter for the next person. You could even let someone in front of you park, when you find yourself with extra time. By doing this you will find that your ideal parking space will just appear again and again and again. Remember the key to all of this is—be relaxed, have knowledge, trust, and yet be confident that the right item will come along at the right time.

Just in case you decide along the way that you need a bigger karmic bank account, my suggestion is to do these things of giving and helping on a consistent, regular basis and the bumps in the road of life actually are much smaller. It's good to give a thorough clean out once or twice a year but to do something regularly creates even flow rather than fits and starts.

One morning I was getting a smoothie for myself and a new and young mother was standing beside me. I looked at her and smiled and told her how beautiful her baby was, as her facial expression was very intense. My thought was to give her some relief from the tension, while standing there waiting. I decided that I needed to buy her what she was going to order. She kept refusing and finally I said, "Sometimes you just need to accept that someone wants to give without anything in return." At last she accepted. I listened to my intuition that she needed to have something unexpected and nice in her day and being a new mom had to be demanding. There's nothing to report on something coming back to me, that I'm aware of, but it certainly made me feel good for the rest of the day. Sometimes karma is about how much you help another—period.

Another story is; one night we were sitting at dinner while two great-grandmotherly ladies sat at a table nearby. One kept getting jostled, she was too far into the aisle and so she moved. All I wanted was to help, but she managed on her own just fine. They were getting their bill and I called our waitress over, asking her to find out, discreetly, how much it was and that I would like to pay it. She gave me the bill and I paid it. I wanted to share some fun, mystery and joy for these women who made it so far in life. They were dressed for a night on town in their beautiful outfits. As they asked who paid their bill, we quickly motioned that we wanted it to be anonymous. Fortunately, we stopped her from spilling the beans. We saw their faces light up hearing them tell the waitress that they would be back, it was their first time to the restaurant. I received pure joy from that situation in giving something unexpected to another and seeing them smile.

The Golden Rule is;
Give and You Shall Receive

When you help others, you are entitled to help. I learned early on that when you are feeling bad and it seems that you can not make that feeling change or shift, the best thing to do is to help someone else. Even if it's just to make someone laugh, you will end up laughing. If you give someone food you will be given food. If you help someone out of a tough spot, you will be helped out of a tough spot. Society often tells us that expecting something in return is not the right thing. But to truly use these materializing techniques to their greatest end, take another view. Give yourself permission and know—it's ok to suggest and be clear about what you wish to have returned to you. It's ok to request a specific time frame that you would like for something to come back to you. It is not necessary to demand this; it is necessary to have clarity, precision, energy, happiness and faith that it will come. Even go so far as to have faith that it has already happened. Overall, it's perfectly in alignment with ease of materializing that you know when and how you want it to show up. So let go, take a breath and keep doing wonderful things for others.

Stories How to Use This Aversion to Your Advantage

Renting my new office space

I had been renting a small office in an unlikely complex of townhouses. There were 4 small offices and I was in the front with a fantastic view and could hear the beautiful sound of the huge fountain. I always had my eye out for another location as things weren't quite right with the management, I couldn't pass on the inexpensive rent or the location, so I stayed. Several events happened that made staying difficult. The first, was that they gave 3 days of notice that we were going to be unable to use our offices for 2 weeks. This was extremely difficult considering I saw clients at this location and booked appointments 1-2 months out. I went with it and it worked out, but things were never quite the same after that. The next thing that happened was that my car was towed by the management for some illogical reason. After discussing this with them and they declared that it was my problem, that afternoon I was given notice to move. At first I was upset but that night, when closing up, I decided in the dark, to look for my next office. This time I would be serious. I found several and wrote down the numbers to call the next day, which I did. But on the way home that next night, I decided to take another route and I saw a "For Lease" sign on a building, that I had always thought would be a great location. I walked in the door of this location and the walls were already a color I had envisioned. The space was exactly what I was in need of in order to grow and provide the type of environment I longed for. Within a week the arrangements were made and the city approved. After 3 weeks I moved in at the price I wanted and in an area that was even closer to my home.

137

Shopping in India

India had long been a place that I'd wished to travel to and visit. I had some trepidation about what I was getting myself into by going but decided it was exactly what I needed. Sometimes just going to a place you know nothing about can make the experience have that much more flavor.

I confirmed all details about the trip but had not heard anything back from the hotel after the original confirmation. I had had a bit of trepidation about what to expect when I arrived. When I landed at the Mumbai airport, I made my way through customs with quite a few sidelong looks. Given that I was one of three blondes in the crowd at 2am, I stood out a little and found that to be true for the balance of the trip. When I walked out of the airport there was a hired car waiting for me and so the trip started off well, trusting that it would all work out.

After a few days, there was a group that got together to see some of the sights and "shop" so I decided to go. It was supposed to be the best place to shop in the city. Everyone was excited. We get there and there were a total of 2 very small buildings with 5 stores. My first thought was, this is it? Well they were the best products but they were definitely the highest prices I'd ever seen. The prices were higher than we'd even pay here in the U.S.

Stories How to Use This Aversion to Your Advantage

It was hot and dripping humid as it was the rainy season and we were by the Bay of Bengal. Traffic was very heavy and the streets difficult to see across let alone walk across. I ducked out of the over-priced air conditioned stores as fast as I could and just stood outside for a few moments, feeling a little bummed out, I decided that this was my only opportunity to get what I wanted to bring back to friends and family. I scanned the street left and right and across. Next thing you know I'm racing across the street away from Prada of India and into a throng of people on the sidewalk, jostling each other as they walked.

What I found were some of the best silk scarves, saris, trinkets, statues, and pillow covers available. I discovered that I'd also found the best prices in India as well. So I began racing through the stands and products down the street because I only had about 40 minutes before we were to leave. One of the items I was so set on was a white cotton Punjabi, which is a 2-piece pant and long top combination. I was set on paying 4 U.S. dollars for it, because I had been told a story before leaving the U.S. that this was possible, for it and in a size that is smaller than most people usually wear. The odds seemed stacked against me to find this specific outfit. Next thing you know I'm at the end of this shopping bonanza and it's a major intersection, with no where else to go, with a palace on one side. I stopped and that was when I saw a bunch of Punjabi outfits and started asking about size and price. I negotiated one down to 3 U.S. dollars and trusted that it fit. Later, I found out that it was the perfect fit.

A Ring

One of my favorite rings had gotten smashed during a move and I was extremely disappointed. I knew that finding a replacement was going to be a challenge. There were many times I thought of looking for one but decided against it. I tried to have one made and it didn't come out the way I wanted. So I decided how much I was willing to spend. Because the original ring had been purchased from gift certificates and discounts, I didn't remember how much had been spent. My mother was coming to visit and we were driving to Colorado for a short vacation. We visited the family there and of course she wanted to take a day trip shopping, oh was I happy about that. So I took her to this rustic town and being a good daughter I tagged along to a few shops. Then I decided that she needed a mission and so I told her about the ring. She dragged me to the front of every shop that had rings and showed me ring after ring after ring. How about that one? How about this one? Finally I said enough let's go get an early dinner and after we'll go back to the hotel. I then saw this one store that had spiritual and earthy items and decided to go in and lo there were rings. So my mother starts her "How about this one?" thing while I ignored her; I already had three on the top of the counter and within minutes picked my replacement ring. Now in this instance I forgot about my spending rule and decided to just say I'll take it. When it was rung up the price was well below the price I had allotted for the ring.

Mini speakers

I was returning home from a trip to the Far East and had a long layover in Japan. One of the people in my group that had an even longer layover was talking about how cheap the electronics were (I'm an electronics and gadget techie) and that he was going into the city to find the best deals. Well I didn't have enough time for a trip into Tokyo and about that time a few others in the group mentioned that there was an underground mall in the airport and there were amazing deals that we should check out. We had a few hours until our plane left, so I said sure. Little did I know that it would take about 45 minutes to get to this mall. My friends were busy buying things and calculating the currency conversion and so I wandered to another store because I was bored. Just as everyone was catching up with me I found some portable speakers that would make teaching easier than what I had been using. I had some difficulty understanding the currency conversion and so it took me a while to decide to purchase them. About the time the purchase was complete I realized that my plane was supposed to leave in about 15 minutes and I was 30 minutes away. I was panicked and ran only to forget my coat at security and had to go back. I kept chanting in my head "It's ok, it's ok, it's ok, it's ok" and kept any negative thinking or worrying from getting into my thoughts. By the time that I got near the area where the plane was boarding, I again heard my name being called. Imagine how that felt I'm in Japan and it was possible that I would have to stay in this stuffy little airport for another day or so if I missed this flight. When I got to the door of the plane, I was told by the gate agent that they held the plane for me. Wow, I was grateful that I didn't miss my flight and once back in the U.S. found that the speakers were double the price and so it was well worth the panic.

A Suit

I was on a business trip in Texas and the trip had gone well except for the food. The food in Texas is definitely not for someone from California who eats light fare, and doesn't like a lot of sauces. At the end of the trip I needed another suit because I had so nicely spilled hot sauce on my suit that I was going to need for my next client visit. So on my way to the airport I saw a "mall" and yes I stopped at the "mall," but given that I only had about 40 minutes to get in, buy something, and get out and make the plane I decided to risk it. I had decided long before that if I ever needed to buy something for a business situation while on the road I was committed to spending a limited amount. The reason for this is that when you're on business and in need of something often you'll pay a premium unless you have some specific limits. I found a great parking spot close to the store entrance and I literally, ran in checked the store legend and raced to the store I knew that had clothes in my size, tried on 3 suits and a blouse and made my purchase of a new designer suit that happened to be in my size, and on sale for an amazing $79. I was out and back in my rental car in 35 minutes. I made my flight and my client never knew about the stained suit. I was clear about the need and it materialized effortlessly.

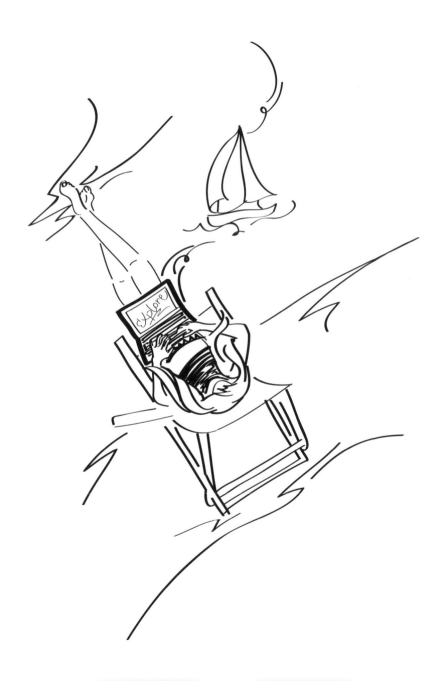

The purpose of this book has been to share my experiences with you using humor and a story. When we are told a story our brain remembers this story and gets set in motion to act on the tools. Through a story you will relate to your own life and can capture the same or better results because of the essence of the story and how it relates to your life.

My hope is that you will understand that materializing and manifesting *is* something as simple as shopping, but as complex as resolving or clearing the energetic obstacles in your mind and physical environment so that you achieve amazing results.

The greatest masters of time used the word alchemy when speaking of materializing. Alchemy is that which is transformed from one element into another. While alchemy is not used often or well in our mainstream society, Paulo Coelho used it wonderfully in his book "The Alchemist." Materializing, in this book, is used like alchemy in our daily lives for simple things. Alchemy can also inspire you. It may inspire you to challenge yourself to bring about much more intricate results. The key to all of this is consistent practice and awareness of what you are intending, along with consistent action. Inconsistency leads to fits and starts. I teach my client's that inconsistent action leads to inconsistent results. Lack of clarity leads to scattered results.

There is more to learn and understand when speaking of alchemy or materializing but this metaphorical approach will take you to very high levels of achievement, even though it may seem like a book of fun and frivolity.

"Shotgun Shopping" is Really Materializing What you Want, Wish, and Desire

Some stories about how these techniques
worked after reading this book:

I just finished reading "Shotgun Shopping" and wanted to let you know how it has helped me, in my life. For over 5 years now, I have been around Sheevaun and have taken all of her classes and workshops. After reading "Shotgun Shopping" I realized that I had forgotten a few key tools that she taught me. One of them being, letting go of items that don't serve me. In this case I had bought, my now ex-boyfriend and myself, a matching pair of PJ's that had cute peppers on them, about 5 years ago. They have been one of my favorite pairs of PJ's because I had washed them so many times. I never wanted to give them away. After reading the book, I realized that by keeping them and wearing them, I would think of him and our relationship every time I had them on. Once I realized this, I decided that I truly wanted to let that part of my life go, so I gave them away to Goodwill the next day, along with other articles of clothes that reminded me of other difficult times in my life.

Thank you Sheevaun! You never stop amazing me with your vast amount of knowledge!!

Sincerely
LMD

"Shotgun shopping" has made me aware of "needs" and "wants". It made me think of the "value" of items I have bought and self value. It is written with humor and personal examples of Sheevaun's shopping experiences. The message in the book is so deep and profound. A step by step of what to do, to achieve everything on your wish list makes it easy to follow. This is so applicable not only to your shopping, but to your career and your life in general. Thank you Sheevaun, for yet again, bringing the complex energies of the universe, simplifying the process and handing it out to all to benefit. Bless you!!!

Doris Siksek Muna
Founder of Dorothea LLC

Sheevaun gave me an advanced copy of the first 2 chapters and just by using those, I had an amazing experience. I went to Costco and couldn't find anyone to help me with the load that I had purchased and I used the techniques to get clear. A few minutes later this big, handsome, guy steps up to me and says he's here to help me with my purchases and will get them to my car for me. I loved using the techniques – they've worked so many times for me that I've lost count.

One who used to overshop and now shops just right.

"Shotgun Shopping" is Really Materializing What you Want, Wish and Desire

Shotgun Shopping

About the Author

Sheevaun O'Connor Moran has written articles for LA Times, Conscious Living, New Age Retailer, AZ NetNews, Travel Journal and Entrepreneur Magazine. She wrote a monthly column for the Grunion Gazette in Long Beach California for 2 years. Ms. Moran has written copy for marketing materials since 1985 and continues to do so for several of her consulting clients.

Sheevaun has a passion for bringing a new way of thinking to the world, and through the writing of "Shotgun Shopping" she has captured the essence of a new way of shopping. She gives new life to old thoughts about materializing and shopping. This will turn the shopping carts sideways and may even create new shopping terminology.

NOTES

NOTES

NOTES

NOTES